GAUDÍ

ALL GAUDÍ

Photographs: Miquel Badia, Oriol Llauradó, Mike Merchant, Luis Miguel Ramos Blanco, Tavisa and FISA-Escudo de Oro, S. A. Photographic Archives.

Text, lay-out, design and printing by
EDITORIAL ESCUDO DE ORO S.A.

Copyright of this edition for photographs and text:
© EDITORIAL ESCUDO DE ORO, S.A.
Palaudàries, 26 - 08004 Barcelona (Spain).
www.eoro.com
e-mail: editorial@eoro.com

I.S.B.N. 84-378-2205-X
Legal Dep. B. 380-2005

LETTER FROM THE EDITOR

Nowadays, and especially after the successful celebration in 2002 of the International Year of Gaudí with the reason of the 150th anniversary of his birth, there are numerous works by Gaudí on the market. Until now, it could be said that there were very few publications, especially when compared with the abundant literature dedicated to other great architects. We feel proud about being one of the first publishers that published a book about the work of Gaudí, specially thought of for the tourist public, widely illustrated and fruit of an exhaustive work of documentation and photography. It was the year 1974, only seven years after Editorial Escudo de Oro had been founded. Since then, there have been many updated reprints or new editions that we have made from this book, which has been edited in seven languages –Spanish, English, French, German, Italian, Japanese and Russian–, our intention being to extend it to many others.

This letter wants to thank the tourist, the tourist of any nationality and condition that throughout these years has come to Catalunya and Barcelona, in particular, to discover in situ, the genius of Gaudí. With you, we have learned to appreciate his magnificent work, his creativity and his influence even more. As Barcelonans, we already feel proud and as a publisher specialized in tourism, we hope to keep feeding this passion we all feel for Gaudí.

Antoni Gaudí in 1878. This photograph, kept in the Reus Museum, is one of the few portraits of the artist that has been preserved. Gaudí, especially towards the end of his life, never liked to pose for journalists.

The President Prat de la Riba and Bishop Reig on a visit to Sagrada Familia, listening to Gaudí giving explanations. Antoni Gaudí in the Corpus Christi procession in ▷ 1924 (flight of stairs of the cathedral in Barcelona).

INTRODUCTION

Antoni Gaudí i Cornet was born on the 25th of June 1852 in Reus although there is speculation about the possibility that he might have been born in Riudoms, a village situated only 4 kilometres away where his parents owned a small house. He was the fifth and last child of Francesc Gaudí i Serra, a boilermaker, and Antònia Cornet i Bertran who also came from a family of boilermakers. This fact was to prove a determining factor in the professional trajectory of Gaudí. It was he himself who said, in his old age, that his sense of space became apparent to him in his father's workshop and with the copper tubes that his father handled. As regard his brothers and sisters, two of them died at a very early age, one at the age of two the other at the age of four. Another of his brothers, Francesc, died for reasons unknown in 1876 shortly after graduating with a degree in Medicine. His death was shortly followed by that of their mother and later his elder sister, Rosa, in 1879, leaving to Gaudí the charge of her little daughter. The little girl and Gaudí's father moved with him to Barcelona. Gaudí's father passed away in 1906 at the age of 93 and his niece an infirm woman who never enjoyed good heath, died in 1912 at the age of 36.

Antoni Gaudí did not enjoy a strong healthy constitution either. As a child he was diagnosed as having rheumatic problems which prevented him from playing with other children although he did go out for long walks, a custom which he continued up until the end of his life. This immobility which he often suffered from sharpened a sense of observation in the young Gaudí leading him to discover, with great fascination, the great spectacle offered by Nature. This was his principal source of inspiration for decorating all of his works and provided him with the solution to many problems that his construction projects posed. In fact his

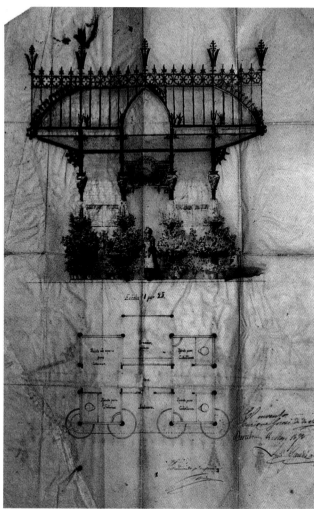

Plan for the public urinals designed in 1878 next to their inventor, Enrique Girossi, considering locating them in the Ramblas. The front part served as a place for flowers, newspapers or drinks whilst the rear is where the urinals are located. The upper part is equipped with a clock, thermometer and barometer and on the sides are the glass cases for advertisements. (Source: I.M.H.B.).

Street lamps plan for the Sea Wall Avenue, 1880.
The project consisted of a total of eight street lamps each one measuring 20 metres in height and with a landscaped platform. Likewise in these were engraved the names of the most important Catalan admirals. (Source: Ràfols).

method of working was inspired by Nature, a process that has come to be known as «organic construction» by which one idea is adds to another and transforms as it grows.

Another important aspect of his childhood noted by many writers, is the fact that he came from the village of Reus, and by association, from the countryside of Tarragona. Tenacity, stubbornness, and strong willed, are characteristic traits associated with the people of Reus and were traits observed in Gaudí himself. It was his tenacity and stubbornness that allowed Gaudí to carry on with his vanguard projects and ideas in the face of opposition. This was even more the case when the greater part of the society in which he lived, including critics and more than one of his clients, did not view positively all that he was trying to do.

Both in the Pares Escolapis school in Reus and the Architecture College in Barcelona, Gaudí did not figure as a brilliant student. But, he was an excellent draughtsman and much of his university work already demonstrated his unusual creativity. The greater part of his preoccupation about art was stimulated by books and his own experience. From the outset of his university career he worked in the offices of various architects as much to learn his profession as to pay his way through university.

At the same time Gaudí took part in various «tertulias» (café society discussion gatherings) which had strong Catalan and even anticlerical tendencies, although the latter contrasts with Gaudí's progressively growing religious beliefs as time passed. Similarly, Gaudí came into contact with workers movements and the concept of cooperative worker efforts of the period. In fact, his first major job was a project for a factory and a workers quarter for the Workers' Cooperative Society of Mataró (1878-1882). Unfortunately the initia-

The Bodegues Güell (Garraf, Barcelona), the work of Francesc Berenguer i Mestres built in 1895 and 1897, a project in which Gaudí collaborated. The influence of Gaudí can be seen above all in the parabolic arches and the ceilings. Likewise, the iron entrance door has a similar appearance as that in the Pavilions Güell.

In 1900 Gaudí accepted the assignment for the Spiritual League of Our Lady of Montserrat to carry out the first of fifteen groups of sculptures corresponding to the «rosary mystery» in the route that goes from the monastery to Holy Cave. However, the idea for the figure of Christ did not meet with approval and for this reason Gaudí abandoned the project. It was finished by J. Llimona.

Entrance porch to Miralles Estate (1901) in Barcelona where a statue had been installed evoking the architect.

tive of this Cooperative Society failed and resulted in only two houses being built.

The city of Mataró also left its mark on Gaudí at a personal level. It was here that the only documented romantic episode related to Gaudí took place. It seems that the affair did not prosper as the girl in question decided in favour of another suitor. And so Gaudí remained a bachelor for the rest of his life, and although the reasons are unknown what is clear is that he buried himself in architecture and his work with a sense of complete dedication.

1878 was a key year in the professional life of Gaudí, it was then that he was awarded the title of architect. He carried out the aforementioned projects for the Obrera Mataronense and the public urinals invented by Enrique Girossi. The Ajuntament of Barcelona (Local Government) charged him with the responsibility of designing a street lamp for the Plaça Reial, and Manuel Vicens put him in charge of what would be his first house. But, most important of all, he met Eusebi Güell i Bacigalupi (1846-1918) who was his main defender and patron.

This rich industrialist had seen a very original glass cabinet designed by the young architect Gaudí in Esteve Comella's glove shop and he was fascinated by the cabinet. He wanted to meet Gaudí and invited him to his house. This was the beginning of a deep friendship and mutual admiration between Güell and Gaudí that continued until Güell's death.

It was this friendship that made possible the creation of some of the works of genius such as the Pavilions Güell, Güell Palace, Park Güell and the Güell Colony crypt. Likewise, Gaudí carried out a project for Güell in 1883, a hunting pavilion in the Garraf region near Sitges, and it is almost certain that he collaborated in the construction of the Bodegues Güell (1895-1897).

For Gaudí, Güell represented the great patron who allowed him to express himself freely and put into practice both the great and small ideas that Gaudí wanted to apply to his creations. In addition to this, the fact that Gaudí became a part of the Güell family circle of friends (they were one of the wealthiest families in Catalonia) in addition to the fact that they were great lovers of the arts and culture, also allowed Gaudí to become acquainted with the crème de la crème of the ruling class. For Güell, Gaudí represented the ideal architect to make an impression on a society and era when the representation of form dominated social life. The ironic comments and criticisms awoken by Gaudí's work did not influence either man. Gaudí always remained faithful to his beliefs regarding his work while Güell always defended his work and, in addition, promoted him in other projects. Prior to his first assignment for Güell (the entrance and pavilions of the Güell estate), Gaudí carried out two interesting constructions, the Casa Vicens and El Capricho. These were works in which a certain historicist style still predominates with an unequivocal influence of Arabic art but, these already bore the personal Gaudí seal. Moreover, in March 1883 Gaudí was given the charge of architect for the Sagrada Familia Temple. He dedicated practically his entire life to this great work of construction, in fact the last twelve years of his life, from 1914 to 1926, he dedicated his time exclusively to this. Whilst in the midst of the construction of Park Güell (1886-1890), Gaudí accepted two new projects: the Episcopal Palace in Astorga (1887-1894) in the province of León, and the St. Teresa of Avila College (1889-1894), in Barcelona. Moreover during the same period we can add another project, the Casa de los Botines (1891-1892), in the city of León. In 1891 he travelled with the second Marquis of Comillas to Malaga and to Tangiers to visit the place where he was to prepare a construction project for a Franciscan Mission. Finally, in 1892, Gaudí began the construction of the Sagrada Familia Nativity facade.

In 1898 he drew up the first sketches for the Güell Colony church although the work did not begin until 1908. During the same year, 1898, he undertook the construction of the Casa Calvet for which, later in 1900, he received the annual award granted by the Local Government for the best building in the city. This was the only award that Gaudí received throughout his entire life as an architect and this was precisely due to the fact that it was the most conventional building he ever designed. Later in 1900 he designed the First Mystery of the Glory for the Monastery of Montserrat. He later abandoned the project due to a strong disagreement with the governing board, and began the so-called Torre Bellesguard and Park Güell. George Collins, art history professor at the University of Columbia, New York, put on a major exhibition of Gaudí's work in New York in 1952 which signified a world-wide recognition of Gaudí as an architect. In his words «Gaudí's break with historicism, which was such a prolific theme in 19th century architecture, began a little after 1900 when he was designing chairs and benches for the Casa Calvet and the pavil-

Xalet del Catllaràs (1905), La Pobla de Lillet. Currently, it is a refuge for hikers managed by the Pere Tarrés Foundation.

ions at the entrance of Park Güell and was beginning to plan out the church for the Güell Colony».

Gaudí's last works are defined by his own peculiar style. Within this category one can include the aforementioned Park Güell (1900-1914) and the Güell Colony crypt (1908-1915), the alterations to the Casa Batlló (1905-1907), the Casa Milà «La Pedrera» (1906-1910) and the Sagrada Familia Temple and its parish schools (1909-1910). One should not forget the restoration of the Majorca Cathedral (1903-1914), a project that he later abandoned; his participation in the Miralles Estate (1901), in Barcelona, where he designed the entrance door and part of the one of the walls; or the sketches that he drew up for the building of the hotel in New York (1908).

To this list, two more works should be added, both done in 1905 in La Pobla de Lillet, in the Pyrenees: the so-called Xalet del Catllaràs and the Artigas Gardens. The Chalet of Catllaràs, today

set aside as a refuge for hikers, originally served as a residence for the doctors of the area mines. The carbon that was extracted from these mines was for a cement factory owned by Güell. While building this Chalet, Gaudí received the commission of the industrialist Joan Artigas for designing a garden on the terrain of his property. In this, a clear influence of Park Güell, a work that he had initiated five years earlier, can be observed. A cylindrical pergola, the railings of the paths, a bridge and an artificial grotto stand out in these gardens.

In the middle of the afternoon on the 7th of June 1926, Antoni Gaudí was taking his usual afternoon stroll to the San Felipe Neri church, and as usual caught up in his own thoughts when he was suddenly run over by a tram. He died three days later. He was buried in the Sagrada Familia crypt, the chapel he loved so much and to which de dedicated himself almost completely in the last years of his life.

Artigas
Gardens, 1905
(La Pobla de
Lillet).

Cascade, Ciutadella Park.

CIUTADELLA PARK CASCADE
(1875-1881). Parc de la Ciutadella, Barcelona.

Although strictly speaking this is not one of Gaudí's works it should be valued among the first projects he participated in. At that time, during the 1870's, Antoni Gaudí was a young student of architecture who, in order to pay for his classes, worked in the offices of various architects such as Francisco de Paula del Villar as well as frequently collaborating with the master builder, Josep Fontseré i Mestres. This master builder,

responsible for the Born Market (1873-1876) and later the Umbracle (1883-1884) which is a building also located in the Ciutadella Park, was the disputed winner of a competition held by the Ajuntament (Local Government) in 1873. This competition was held to invite entries for the planning of this new space which had been recovered for the city as a public park. Up until then this space was where a foreboding fortress stood until it was demolished in 1869. It had been built under the instructions of King Felipe V after having laid siege on Barcelona in 1714 with the idea of securing military control of the city. In addi-

tion to this, Josep Fontseré was also given the charge of designing a new waterfall monument next to the artificial lake. The neoclassic conception of this monument contrasts with the naturalism with which various decorative elements were resolved and it is precisely here where one can attribute the direct influence of Gaudí, at least in their design. One can suppose an extensive collaboration of the young Gaudí in the remaining works by Fontseré in his park development project such as entrance gates and ironwork and the so-called Building of Waters with a large lake in the terrace roof to supply water to the entire enclosure.

Street lamp, Plaça Reial.

THE PLAÇA REIAL STREET LAMPS
(1878-1879). Plaça Reial, Barcelona.

During the era when the old Barcelona was undergoing a profound urban transformation immediately after the demolition of the city walls in 1854, there was debate concerning how to go about the urban planning of the Eixample district. Finally, in 1860, the government approved the plan by Ildefons Cerdà and land was laid out for the Plaça Reial. This plaza was constructed between 1850 and 1860 over the old land of the Capuchin Convent which had been handed over to the city. Francesc Daniel Mora was the architect who won the competition for this project. The landscaping of this elegant and spacious frame structure was not definitively drawn up until 1878 which was the year that the Local Government charged Gaudí with the task of designing a street lamp to illuminate this space.

Of the two plans presented the one that was carried out was one consisting of two street lamps each with six arms that open out like the branches of a tree. Despite being so young, Gaudí demonstrated a mastery of the materials used in this small project (the constructive rationality is a constant theme in all of his work) by integrating the ornamental elements into the actual construction.

The plaza was remodelled in 1984 by the architects Correa and Milà who substituted the flowerbeds and traffic zone for a continual pavement whilst respecting the street lamps designed by Gaudí, the Three Graces fountain and the palm trees. On the Avenue of Marquès d'Argentera, number 2, in front of the Civil Government building, we find two more Gaudí lampposts. They were installed in the year 1890 and are the models with three arms.

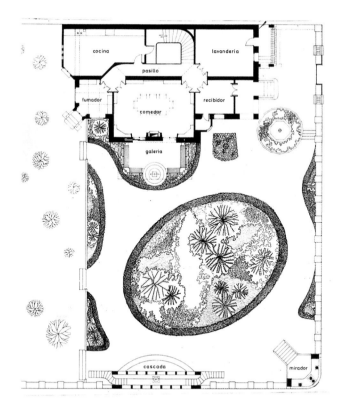

General design for Casa Vicens with the lower floor according to Gaudí's plan (Source: Bergós).

Casa Vicens from the garden, as constructed by Gaudí (Source: A.H.U.A.D.).

CASA VICENS
(1878-1885). Carrer de les Carolines 18-24, Barcelona. Privately owned residence.

In this, the first of Gaudí's grand projects, he already revealed his peculiar genius as an architect and his extravagant sense of fantasy as an artist. The house looks as if it has been taken straight from a fairytale and, bearing this in mind, we have to imagine what the garden would have looked like in its original format as it was significantly modified during extensive alterations carried out in 1925. Also, we need to take into account the widening of the Carrer de les Carolines and the sale of the greater part of this in 1946 and 1962 when two neighbouring houses were erected. If we look at the general lines of the house and the garden as Gaudí planned them, we can see that the principal entrance gave out on to the street perpendicular to the Carrer de les Carolines. The garden is the part that has almost completely disappeared and it is the same story for many of its ornamental elements, such as the part of the wall, a summerhouse and a cascade.

Casa Vicens was built between 1883 and 1885, although Gaudí drew up the plans for it in 1878, the same year he was awarded the title of architect. The young architect was hired by Manuel Vicens, who manufactured bricks and ceramic tiles, to design a summer residence. So, this represents the artist's first important job and in particular his first house project. At the same time Gaudí continued to dedicate time to the planning of the Mataró Cooperative and it was also during this time that he met Eusebi Güell and entered into collaboration with the architect Joan Matorell. At the latter's proposal in March 1883, Gaudí began to work on the Sagrada Familia Temple succeeding Francisco de Paula del Villar. The ground plan of the house is essentially rectangular whose form is broken by the advance towards the dining room garden and by the lesser dimensions of the so-called smoking room. Nevertheless, Gaudí managed to bestow this simple ground plan with a complex titration thanks to the rich conception of the facades. This facade abounds with

Casa Vicens today seen from Carrer de les Carolines.

Bar of the entrance, which imitate palm leaves.

Detail of the windows.

Details of the balconies. In each corner of the building, half way up, a small tower with a balcony.

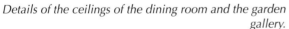

Details of the ceilings of the dining room and the garden gallery.

Door for going out into the garden from the smoking room whose ceiling is decorated with a concave ardornment.

projections be they small towers or balconies. In order to achieve this, he used stone as the base element combined with bricks and the entire piece is covered with multiple coloured ceramic tiles which were materials closely associated with the building's owner.

As regards the ornamentation and the architectural aspect of the house, Gaudí was principally inspired by the Mudejar Art. But, one can also catch a glimpse of a constant search for, and application of, new architectural forms and ornamental elements. In a way Gaudí just like Lluís Domènech i Montaner with the Montaner i Simon Publishers (1879-1886, today the headquarters of the Antoni Tàpies Foundation), heralded a new era in architecture, Modernism, which clearly contrasted with the majority of the buildings of the period that were examples of an eclectic Classicism. Furthermore, his concept of architec-

tural works as a whole where one cannot overlook any detail was already patently obvious in his first project. It was the very same Gaudí who designed the original iron railings for the entrance, the windows, of the exquisite and profuse decoration of the dining room, and the smoking room. In short, each corner leaves one with a sense of his strong personality and at the same time creates a clearly different ambience in each space.

EL CAPRICHO

EL CAPRICHO
(1883-1885). Comillas (Cantabria). Privately owned residence, since 1988 the location of a restaurant.

As was the case for Casa Vicens, the reminiscences of Arabic Art are striking in El Capricho which is the name by which this small palace has been known, constructed in Comillas by Gaudí for Don Máximo Díaz de Quijano. Here, Gaudí returned to using ceramic tiles as a decorative element although his theme, a sunflower, is more indigenous to the region. Here, one is also reminded of Arabic Art with the slender tower in the form of a minaret which rises up in one of the extremes above the portico of the main entrance and which bestows the entire piece with a great elegance. Nevertheless, in comparison with the Casa Vicens, El Capricho appears to the viewer like a less dreamlike work with a more austere decoration. On the other hand, the ground plan of the building is already more arbitrary.

It was conceived as a summerhouse for a wealthy bachelor such as was Máximo Díaz de Quijano. Gaudí paid special attention to the lounge, a space for social interaction, which has a large window and two small balconies of unusual height providing it with a greater dimensions. Distributed around this principal room are the antechamber, the dining room and the bedrooms for guests whilst the kitchen and the servants bedrooms are located in the ground floor and semibasement. Finally, the third level of the building is where the attic is situated. Due to the marked unevenness of the terrain, Gaudí made use of stone like a pedestal base which raises the entire structure and is where the

Western and southern façade.

Details of the windows.

semi-basement level is placed. In the south face he erected a containing wall adorned in harmony with the house. Between this wall and the building itself he sited a plaza which was conceived for open air social gatherings. Máximo Díaz de Quijano did not manage to live to enjoy the fruits of this construction work as just before the construction was finished he met an untimely death.

El Capricho was one of the few Gaudí buildings where he did not carry out his habitual practice of constantly overseeing the project. This practice allowed him to transform the initial plans into the actual development of the construction and maintain a constant dialogue with the workers and artisans to determine and control all of the details. One needs to take into account that at the same time El Capricho was being constructed, Gaudí, who was in Barcelona, was embarking on various projects such as the Casa Vicens, the Sagrada Familia Temple and the pavilions for the Finca Güell. In the case of El Capricho we know that Gaudí visited the terrain at least once and that he was in constant contact with the architect who he assigned to the construction. His name was Cristòfol Cascante i Colom who had studied with Gaudí at university and worked in the same offices of the master builder Josep Fontseré. Cristòbal Cascante had already carried out some work in the Cantabria zone. In addition to the elegant tower that presides over the entire construction and original entrance porch, other noteworthy aspects are the large sash windows that, when operated, emit musical notes, and the work of forging the balustrades of some of the small balconies with metallic tubes that also give off sounds when the windows are opened or closed.

*General view
of the
entrance to
«El Capricho».*

Aerial view of the Güell Pavilions.

THE FINCA GÜELL PAVILIONS

(1884-1887). Avinguda de Pedralbes 7, Barcelona. Since 1977, the headquarters of the Gaudí Chair.

The first task that Eusebi Güell hired Gaudí for, a hunting pavilion in the lands that he owned in the municipality of Garraf near Sitges, was a pro-

ject that never went beyond paper. This was 1883. That same year, however, Güell charged him with a new assignment. The Güell summerhouse which was in Les Corts de Sarrià, at that time in the outskirts of Barcelona, had just been extended as a result of the purchase of adjoining lands and Güell wanted Gaudí to design a wall that would embrace the entire

property. This wall was to provide three entrances, one main entrance and two secondary, in addition to some alterations to the house itself and other elements of the garden. The old main entrance to the Güell Estate is the work that was so original that we can still contemplate today and which includes the celebrated Dragon Gate. To the left is the porter's

24

Entrance door to the Güell Pavilions.

The famous winged dragon at the entrance to the Güell Estate.

Two aspects of the building of the ▷
caretaker's office.

lodge, and to the right the stables and the riding school. The rest of the estate was significantly altered after the death of Güell.

On the one hand the opening of the Avinguda Diagonal in 1919 divided this extensive property. The house and part of the gardens were a gift to the Spanish Royal family, trans-

forming the house, between 1919 and 1924 in what today is the Royal Palace of Pedralbes. On the other hand, in 1950 the Universitat de Barcelona acquired various terrains to build the new University City. These terrains included the pavilions at the entrance to the Güell Estate which in 1977 sheltered the Gaudí

Chair a branch of the Escola Tècnica Superior d'Arquitectura de Barcelona de la Universitat Politècnica de Catalunya. The other two entrances to the estate designed by Gaudí were much simpler. Having now lost their practical purpose, they were demolished, although one of them was rebuilt in 1953 and today one can

Dome of the riding school, grille of a side door and the top of the column next to the main door, inspired by the branches of an orange tree.

contemplate it close by Pharmacy Faculty.

There is no doubt that the most outstanding and eye-catching aspect of the Güell Pavilions is the large door with its notable dragon. This was made from wrought iron, measures five metres in length and is supported on one side by a brick column that reaches ten metres in height. The expressive nature of the dragon is such that is seems as if the door had been designed solely to create this dragon spectacle. Its aggressive demeanour fulfils perfectly its mission of a creature that jealously guards the extensive estate that opens up behind it. The

Detail of the wall and bell of the main door.

symbolic value of this creature is transmitted to the Garden of the Hesperides and can be identified with the dragon Ladon that was chained by Hercules. To this symbolic order we must also include the oranges at the pinnacle of the column that supports the door and the position of the dragon's body which is the same as the stars that make up the Dragon and Hercules constellations. The figure of the dragon was one of Gaudí's favourite themes although no other work quite captures the monumental nature of the one here. The question of the building of the two pavilions that finish off the entire work was resolved by Gaudí with great economy of means as one can see by looking at the materials used. This emphasises once again Gaudí's dedication to details regarding construction and ornamentation even though such details may seem insignificant. The exterior decoration, which combines coloured ceramics, brick and a set of relief work on the walls, still leave one with a sense of a certain influence from Arab Art, although here Gaudí left his most personal mark in relation to the two earlier works, the Casa Vicens and El Capricho.

In contrast to the profuse exterior decoration the interior of the stables, the riding school and the porter's lodge all make up clean and very functional spaces. The porter's lodge has three bodies, the principal one with an octagonal ground plan with a lowered dome. The stable building is a prolonged construction solely defined by a succession of arches with parabolic outlines. The riding school, a pavilion next to the stables, is fashioned in a circular form with an upper gallery and a dome which lets in natural light. These buildings, the porter's lodge, the stables and the riding school, are separated by the entrance door, or the Dragon, although they are stylistically united by their exterior decoration and the small towers which they all end in.

The construction of the Güell Pavilions took place at the same time as the Güell Palace, the work beginning in 1886. However, both construction works represent quite different architectural worlds as do the purposes of each one.

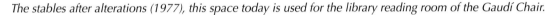

The stables after alterations (1977), this space today is used for the library reading room of the Gaudí Chair.

GÜELL PALACE

Entry gates to the palace. In the centre, the porter's lodge window grille.

GÜELL PALACE
(1885-1890) Carrer Nou de la Rambla 3-5, Barcelona. The headquarters of the «Amics de Güell» Association.

This is a site measuring 18 by 22 metres, a somewhat limited space for erecting what was to be a grand palace for the Güell family. It was to be their city dwelling where they would celebrate their many social gatherings and cultural soirées. In addition, it was to be located in a very narrow street in the centre of the city, and so Gaudí planned out a

magnificent construction from a spatial point of view creating a very complex space in the interior which gives us the impression of finding ourselves in a much larger palace. The Güell Palace takes up some 2,000 m² of ground space and consists of six floors to which we can add the terrace roof treated as another space in the building. A good number of chimneys and vent shafts emerge from the terrace roof that are camouflaged with imaginative coverings made up of tiles and other materials. These sculptures were a prelude to

later terrace roof designs that Gaudí used in the Casa Batlló and Casa Milà.
The white stone facade and sober lines are defined by the first floor gallery and two enormous parabolic arched doors. They were conceived on a large scale to allow carriages to enter as far as the basement where the stables are located. Both doors are decorated with iron grilles upon which the initials of the owner are drawn in the upper part. Between the doors there is an artistic window, corresponding to the porter's lodge, finished off with a kind of column that is also

Güell Palace main facade in Carrer Nou de la Rambla.

Palace basements, in old designated to be the stables.

made of wrought iron where one can see the emblem of Catalonia inscribed.

The interior of the palace is organised around the great first floor room, or suite for social functions. This room is like an interior patio which rises up to the third floor and culminates in a dome that is perforated with multiple circular orifices that give the sensation of standing beneath a starry sky. The lobby, the central focus of the house, which gives on to all the other rooms is where the Güell family held all their social gatherings and presents the viewer with a vision of exquisite decorative wealth and carefully

Vestibule steircase.

Two aspects of the living room-dining room which gives out on to the main facade.

The living room-dining room. ▷

worked details. One example is the organ that Güell had built, its pipes are located in the upper gallery so that the music resonates from above.

The rest of the rooms, although they have a secondary function were not overlooked in the slightest. The variety of ceilings, windows, doors and numerous other elements that make up the palace can be equally admired. All of them were exquisitely designed and rendered by notable artisans and demonstrate the extraordinary imaginative mind of Gaudí.

One of the structural elements that most captures one's attention are the 127 columns of various forms and sizes which unite the building as whole. There are those in the basement that are thick and sturdy. This is where the stables of old can be found and their characteristics are due to the role they play as supporting columns. Then there are the elegantly finished columns in the suite for social functions. All in all, there are forty different types of columns.

Other suggestive corners of the building are also worthy of mention. There are the smoking gallery, the service hanging staircase, the spiral access ramps to the basement where the horses and carriages were taken, the coffered ceilings in the dining room, and artistic pieces such as the small table in the bathroom off the suite for social functions. Alternatively, there is the closet chapel in the main lobby, or the already cited composition of sculptures that Gaudí created with the chimneys and vent shafts on the terrace roof. On the rear facade Gaudí designed an original gallery with blinds that appear to be crowned with an shelter of foliage with undulating shapes.

The construction of the palace was carried out between 1886 and 1890 whilst Gaudí finished the Güell Pavilions and began the project for the St. Teresa of Avila

Vestibule dome, of the first floor large room perforated with multiple circular holes.

College. The palace remained Eusebi Güell's residence until 1906. Later, in 1954, the building was acquired by the County Council of Barcelona which undertook the task of restoration always respecting the original building. In 1984, along with Park Güell and the Casa Milà, the palace was declared part of the Heritage to Humanity by UNESCO. With this extraordinary and audacious construction work, in which everything is incredibly creative and whose unique style differed so much from the majority of buildings constructed during the same period, Gaudí began to become acknowledged. He awoke interest among the media and various articles were written about him.

The vestibule or large hall of the first floor was planned as an interior patio.

Rear façade.

The Güell Palace terrace roof made up of a lovely garden of chimneys. Each one takes on a different shape and practically all of them are covered in coloured ceramics.

Main facade of the St. Teresa of Avila College.

ST. TERESA OF AVILA COLLEGE
(1888-1889). Carrer Ganduxer 95-105, Barcelona. Private College.

In 1888, Father Enric d'Ossa i Cervelló, founder of the Society of Santa Teresa de Jesús and dedicated to teaching, hired Gaudí to finish off the partially built St. Teresa of Avila College. At the time Gaudí was in the middle of the Güell Palace project. The identity of the previous architect is unknown and had abandoned the construction of the College having only overseen the building of the ground floor. This was a somewhat unusual assignment for Gaudí.

Until now his projects had been limited to private residences for the bourgeoisie carried out with ample budgets, but the assignment for the Order of St. Teresa was determined by a very small budget in line with the profession of apostolic poverty observed by the Order in addition to the observation of moderation and sobriety at all levels of their life. All together this obliged Gaudí to abstain from all kind of baroque ornamentation and bind himself to the demands of austerity set out by the owner and the purpose of the building as a learning centre. It is precisely here where our interest lies in the St. Teresa of Avila College as it constitutes a mag-

nificent example of construction rationality, and yet at the same time is a very personal piece, even more so taking into account that the building had already been started by another architect.

On top of the existing 60 meter long rectangular ground floor, Gaudí erected a further three floors. To carry out the construction Gaudí used inexpensive materials, such as brick, and resolved the general question the building's construction on the basis of parabolic arches and reducing the decorative elements almost exclusively to pragmatic construction solutions. Bearing this in mind, what needs to be underlined here are the long symmetrical passages on the first floor,

*Entrance gate
to the College,
in the bay
window
porch, made
of wrought
iron.*

Detail of the gallery and one of the building corners where the coat of arms of the Carmelite order is inscribed.

one the most magical spaces created by Gaudí. These are narrow passages with profound perspectives obtained by a succession of parabolic arches lit by natural light that sifts through from the interior patio and the white of the limestone confers upon them an special radiance. On the principal facade, and to gain a certain presence, Gaudí added a small projecting building, something like an enclosed balcony or bay window and which has the function of a porch in the lower part. This porch is enclosed by a splendid grating and wrought iron door which symbolically represents the iconography of the order of Santa Teresa de Jesús. In the centre of this enclosed balcony is the order's coat of arms which is a motif that can also be found on the upper corners of the building. All of the facades present the viewer with a sense of harmony created by their lineal form. In the lower floor the openings are defined by parabolic arches; in the first and second floors rectangular shapes predominate, and in the upper floor various sized pointed arches open up. This linear harmony is broken in the enclosed balcony with a different variety of pointed arches that are more rectangular. As a finish to the building, there is an elegant succession of crests and crenellations, and in each of the corners there are pinnacles or small towers that culminate in a cross. Another decorative element on the facades are the sides between the upper floors where an anagram for Jesus is repeated on ceramic plaques. The decorative element that has not survived until today were the birettas that adorned the roof crenellations.

View of the first floor passages, a succession of parabolic arches.

First floor dining room.

EPISCOPAL PALACE OF ASTORGA

(1887-1893). Astorga, León. The headquarters of the Santiago Trail Museum.

In 1887, Gaudí was given the task of erecting the new headquarters for the diocese of the city of León. The former building had been completely destroyed in a fire. The person who charged Gaudí with this task was the bishop of Astorga, Joan B. Grau i Vallespinós, a friend of the architect and also from the same home town, Reus. Gaudí happily accepted the assignment and the same year presented his first sketches which enthused the bishop.

However, before the project could get underway it also required the approbation of the Fine Arts Academy of San Fernando in Madrid who received the project with reservation and asked for some changes to be made. Gaudí met this challenge with his habitual disposition but the Academia would not give ground. After modifying his plans twice to appease the desires of the Academia, in 1889 construction began, although there were discrepancies between Gaudí and the Diocese Board with the exception of Bishop Grau. This lack of agreement continued throughout the entire construction process of the palace.

But, as a result of the death of bishop Grau in 1893, the construction came to an immediate halt. The upper floor and the roof were still to be finished. When construction was supposed to resume there was a lack of understanding and agreement between Gaudí and the Diocese Board which finally ended in the architect's irrevocable resignation. Even later, in 1905, when the new bishop of Astorga pleaded with him to return and finish the building, Gaudí refused offering the excuse that the work involved in the construction of the Sagrada Familia impeded him from doing so. As a result, the architect Ricardo García Guerreta finished the palace. His idea for the roof was quite different from that designed by Gaudí and consisted of a crown in the form of a pyramid, grey-white in colour like the facades in which there were multiple windows. Finally, in 1915, the Episcopal Palace was finished although it never came to be used as a headquarters for the diocese. During the Spanish Civil War it was used as a barracks for the artillery and suffered a series of damages. At the beginning of the 1960's it was restored and in 1963 inaugurated as the headquarters for the Santiago Trail Museum.

One of the outstanding features of the palace is its castle-like appearance. This is reinforced as much by circular towers, buttresses and the small moat that surrounds the entire building, as the use of white granite as the principal construction material, taken from the nearby county of Bierzo. Although this palace has often been criticised for the way it contrasts with the roseate of the neighbouring cathedral, this grey-white colour can be identified with the clothing of the bishops and is in harmony with the winter snow that covers the ground in this region. Clearly inspired by gothic architecture the palace has a Greek Cross ground floor and is organised around a large central space the performs a distributive function.

*Main facade
of the palace.*

45

Casa de los Botines main facade.

CASA DE LOS BOTINES
(1891-1892). Plaza de San Marcelo, León.
Since 1929, the head office of a bank.

In 1891, in mid construction of the Episcopal Palace in Astorga and the recently finished Güell Palace and the St. Teresa of Avila College, Gaudí has hired by Simón and Mariano Andrés, fabric merchants who had their business in León. The assignment was to erect a large building in the centre of the city that would meet their commercial needs as well as acting as a living residence and with other flats that they would rent out. Gaudí's pro-

posals were approved at the end of 1891 and work began immediately. The fact that the company founder was called Joan Homs Botinás caused the building to be popularly known as the Casa de los Botines (the play on his surname rendering «botines» has the meanings of «plunder» or «leggings»!).

Gaudí laid out a building that openly

Two details of the Casa de los Botines: window and grille, St. George and the Dragon.

faced the four winds. The principal facade faced on to the San Marcelo plaza, and this main facade was presided over by a sculpture of St. George and the Dragon, one of Gaudí's favourite themes. The sculpture was moulded in plaster by Llorenç Matamala and sculpted in León by Cantó. The basement opens on to the street to allow in natural light and the ground floor was assigned as a warehouse for fabrics and for the offices. The first floor was assigned as living quarters for the owners, the second and third floors consisted each of four flats to be rented out, and finally, the attic. The entire building is finished off with a two-sided sloping slate tile roof.

The Casa de los Botines is characterised by its sobering structure made of stone. The sensation of solidness that the building gives is only broken graceful and elegant towers that rise up from each corner. Likewise, the ornamental aspects are limited to these towers, a sculpture on the principal entrance and windows with a clearly gothic influence.

General view of the area around the church.

SAGRADA FAMILIA TEMPLE
(1883-1926). Plaça de la Sagrada Familia, Barcelona.

Gaudí dedicated more than forty years of his life to this great and still unfinished work, in fact he dedicated the last twelve years of his life exclusively to it between the years 1914-1926 declining any other project put before him. He even he moved to live within the precincts of this church. This allowed him to work just as he liked: he could remain as close to the construction work for the maximum amount of time resolve any questions that could come up and discuss the different solutions to be put into effect with the workers. Given the lengthy duration of this project it is the one which best illustrates the different steps in the evolution of Gaudí's architecture. For the same reason it is the most difficult of his projects to explain. We decided to introduce this construction project between the two buildings in León and the Casa de Calvet, discussed later. That is to say between 1892 and 1900 when the facade of the Nativity was erected, although the first of its bell towers (and also the only one that Gaudí saw finished known as San Bernabé) was not finished until 1925. The fact that this church took so long to build was due as much to the actual dimen-

Nativity facade.

Old photograph of the schools where one can appreciate the curvature of the outer wall and the roof.

sions of the building as to the resolve of the founders, the Association of Devout Followers of St. Joseph, that this church be solely funded by donations. This last fact meant that work came to a halt on more than one occasion due to the lack of money and it is a well-known anecdote that Gaudí himself helped in fund raising activities on various occasions.

In addition to the facade of the Nativity, part of the construction overseen by Gaudí until his death in 1926 included the crypt, the apse, and a section of the cloister, the part corresponding to the Virgin of the Rosary vestibule.

In the year 2002, the school building was moved next to the façade of the Passion in order to allow the continuation of the work of the central nave. Heavily destroyed by a fire in 1936, the current building is a replica of the one designed by Gaudí. Currently, it forms part of the temple museum.

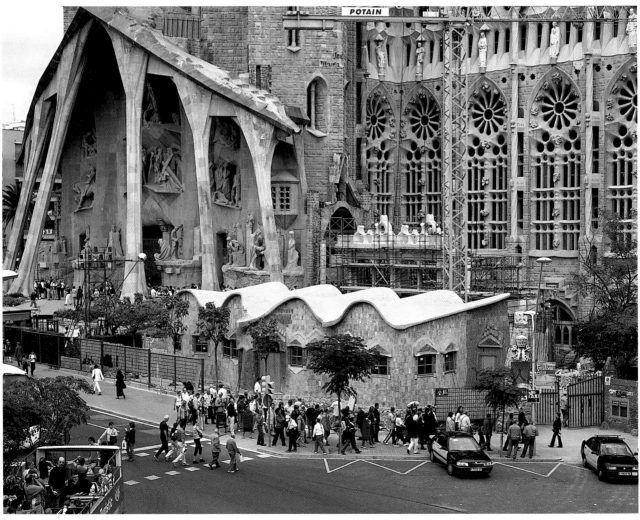

Passion facade, with sculptures by J. M. Subirachs, and the process of constructing the naves.

Pinnacles of the apses: detail of the tops.

But, we must also include the so-called temple schools, built between 1909 and 1910 in the place to be occupied by the principle facade as a foretaste of what future parochial schools should be. And even though this was a provisional building it is really exceptional. It employs the minimum of materials with only simple partition walls conveniently curved and an undulating roof. All of these elements allowed for doing away with load bearing walls without losing structural strength. In the interior there are three rooms divided by two walls that have no real function from a construction point of view, easily transforming the building with a prevailing sense of functionality above all. After Gaudí's death the bell towers of the Nativity facade were finished. A little later, during the Spanish Civil War, the church was the victim of a fire which resulted in the loss of many drawings and plaster models that Gaudí kept in his workshop. Construction work began again in 1954 on the west facade, known as the Passion and where today the part of the naves and roofs have been erected.

Sagrada Familia has a Latin Cross basilica ground floor with five naves longitudinally and three in the transept. The apse is very spacious and is made up of seven chapels with an ambulatory that surrounds the presbytery. A cloister surrounds the building and links the three major access facades. Gaudí maintained the original layout of the church in accordance with the plans of Francisco de Paula del Villar, the temple's first architect and who abandoned the project due to disagreements in 1884 when the crypt was practically finished. However, it should be borne in mind that he would have gone

The crypt's central nave.

Cloister: two views of the Rosary portal.

for a diagonal layout following the modernist idea of singling out to the maximum each part of the city. Likewise, Gaudí completely changed the plans for a neogothic church drawn up by Villar, not only at an aesthetic level but also in terms of its monumental character. This monumental character was based, above all, on the verticality as illustrated by the temple crown. A total of 18 towers: four of them measuring between 98 and 112 metres for each of the three facades representing the twelve apostles; five above the transept, representing Jesus surrounded by the four evangelists, the former rising up to 170 metres in height; and a finally the bell tower covering the apse dedicated to the Virgin Mary.

The crypt was completed by Gaudí in 1885. With regard to the construction work on the crypt already begun by Villar, Gaudí raised the vault so that some of the large windows could illuminate this space decorating it with a beautiful dome keystone over the Annunciation of Mary. He also introduced a channel around it to safeguard against humidity and allow for greater lighting.

The apse was built between 1891 and 1895 in the neogothic style. The most

*Side columns
and vaults
under
construction.*

Facade of the Birth: hallway of the Hope, hallway of the Faith and angels announcing Christmas with their trumpets.

interesting aspect here are the decorative elements of the pinnacles and the gargoyles inspired by fauna and flora that can be seen in the temple's surrounding area: lizards, spirals...

With regard to the cloister the most outstanding feature is the originality of its layout surrounding the entire building. As an example of what could be done with the cloister, Gaudí wanted to finish one part of it, this is the stretch corresponding to the Rosary vestibule next to the Nativity facade with its rich symbolic decoration.

The vestibule dedicated to the Virgin of the Rosary was finished in 1899. But, without a doubt the best work that Gaudí did in the church was the Nativity facade. It is made up of three vestibules which symbolise the three theological virtues: Faith, Hope and Charity, all of them displaying a profusion of sculptures more realist than artistic to illustrate in a didactic manner the various moments in the life of Christ. To the left in the Esperanza (Hope) vestibule are representations of Mary and Joseph's betrothal, the Flight to Egypt and the

Slaughter of the Innocents. In the pinnacle is a rock from the mountain of Montserrat bearing the inscription «Salveu-nos» (Save us). In the vestibule to the right, Fe (Faith) are illustrations of the Visitation, Jesus among the priests in the temple and Jesus as the worker in the carpentry workshop. In the central vestibule there is the scene of the birth of Christ below the star from the East with the Epiphany. Above there are angels announcing the birth with their trumpets, then the Annunciation and the Crowning of Mary. The central vestibule

Central hallway: sculptural door of the Sagrada Familia.

culminates in a cypress tree that represents the Church as a refuge for the faithful who are symbolised by birds with all of this finished off with a cross. In the inner part, and in contrast to the baroque style of the exterior, the Nativity facade is characterised by its simple volumes and pure geometrical forms.

The bell towers emerge from the vestibules and rise up to a height of 100 metres. They are spiral structures, an outward expression of the spiral staircases that wind up along their interiors. In the empty spaces at the highest point of the bell towers, Gaudí foresaw placing tubular bells. This sound would combine with that of the five organs inside the church and with the 1,500 voices of the choir that would extend along both sides of the nave and the wall of the Glory facade. Along the final section of each bell tower you can read «Hosanna Excelsis». Finally, as a finish to the towers there are some geometric figures of colourist notes that symbolise the apostles represented by Episcopal signs: the ring, mitre, crosier and the cross.

The other two facades contain verses about the death and resurrection of

Terminal of a belfry.

Upper part of the central hallway.

Spiral staircase of one of the Nativity facade belltowers and interior of a belltower.

Christ. The first, the Passion, was designed by Gaudí in 1911. Its construction began in 1952 and its sculptures were assigned to Josep Maria Subirachs in 1986. Concerning the main facade, Glory, Gaudí left a study of masses and structures and an iconographic and symbolic plan. With regard to the naves and vaults, around 1910 Gaudí carried out a new project which incorporated applied solutions to the chapel that he had used in the Güell Colony. The final result «will be like a forests» to quote Gaudí's own words, and this would highlight tree-like form columns allowing the light to enter in abundance through the large windows a varying heights.

Casa Calvet main facade.

CASA CALVET
(1898-1900). Carrer Casp 48, Barcelona.
Privately owned housing.

This is a typical middle class house in the Eixample district of Barcelona that Gaudí designed for the widow of Pere Mártir Calvet i Carbonell, manufacturer of fabrics. Its structure follows the habitual distribution of the period: basement, and ground floor for commercial needs, first floor as the living quarters for the owners and the remaining floors to be rented out. At a structural and construction level it is the most conventional of Gaudí's buildings. For this reason it is significant that it is also the only building for which Gaudí's was awarded a prize. The prize was annually awarded by the

Rear façade.

Balcony over the main entrance. In the lower part you can make out the letter «C», the initial of the building's owner.

Entrance lobby mirror where the wooden bench is reflected that was also designed by Gaudí. In contrast, the walls are finished off with blue ceramics.

Two details of the main door: bells and doorknocker where you can see the figure of a beetle.

Detail of a door.

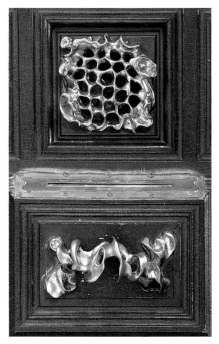

Entry floor: lift and access staircase to the flats.

The old offices of Calvet House today house a restaurant.

Local Government of Barcelona for the best building in the city and was awarded to Gaudí in 1900. Clearly, his architectural ideas were considered far too imaginative to be taken seriously by the official organisations at that time.

At a stylistic level, Gaudí, in the case of Casa Calvet, suppresses all medieval or gothic evocations that are so present in his earlier works. Here he tended towards the options offered by the baroque style, which he had already tried out in the Nativity facade of Sagrada Familia. The references to this style are, above all, evident in the main facade and the entrance lobby, whilst the other facade, which gives on to the back patio, is surprising for its symmetry, something unusual in the work of Gaudí.

The major interest in Casa Calvet resides particularly in secondary elements that, like all of Gaudí's works, were very carefully studied and designed by the architect himself and carried out by notable artisans. There is, for example, in each of the two doors that give entry to the building, a curious knocker below which is hidden an insect which was a symbol of evil due to its bite that caused infection. In this way, the visitor, in order to gain access to the house, symbol-ically drove away evil by striking the insect with the doorknocker. The form of the columns that flank the main door are inspired by the old reels used in the textile industry which was the business of the building's owner.

Other allusions to the building's owner can be found in the gallery on the first floor such as: the initial of the surname; the representation of mushrooms in reference to the owner being an aficionado of botany; the building crown with three effigies that are identified with St. Peter the Martyr the Calvet saint, and the two Gines saints patron saints of Vilassar the home town

*Lower floor office chairs and sofa,
designed by Gaudí in oakwood.*

of the Calvets. In the first floor gallery there are also a representations of a cypress tree (symbol of hospitality), an olive tree, the Catalan coat of arms and the horn of plenty.

The extensive range of magnificent furnishings designed by Gaudí for the Casa Calvet offices were made from oak wood and with organic shapes. Some of these have been recovered and can be contemplated in the same space as the old offices, today fitted out as a restaurant. Likewise, other elements have been respected with regard to the original, such as the panelling that separates the different offices, the counter, handles or old inscriptions. The entrance lobby is also worthy of mention, in particular the exquisite lift which was worked in wood and wrought iron where Gaudí expressed his fantasy world with all kinds of shapes and drawings.

Detail of the lower floor office sofa.

CASA FIGUERAS OR BELLESGUARD

Entrance to Casa Bellesguard.

CASA FIGUERAS OR BELLESGUARD

(1900-1902). Carrer Bellesguard 16-20, Barcelona.
Privately owned residence.

This is situated on the slope of Tibidabo, an enclave from which one has a beautiful panoramic view of Barcelona, hence the name Bellesguard which means «beautiful view». It is also the site where the last Catalan monarch, Martí I l'Humà, had his summer residence built. The extinction of this dynasty and other vicissitudes of history, ended with the abandoning and final disappearance of this old palatial residence. The only remaining witnessing relic being part of the battlement wall and the remains of two of the towers. When Maria Sagués, widow of Jaume Figueras, charged Gaudí with the project of building Bellesguard in 1900, Gaudí himself was inspired by the illustrious past of this historical place. The result of his work was this small and elegant house for a single family and whose style evokes the old medieval castles in what is clearly paying homage to the Catalan gothic style.

In the construction of this house Gaudí wasted no time in making use of the remains of the old mansion that were used in the entrance lobby. The rest of the materials used mainly came from the area around the house thus achieving a high degree of harmony with the surrounding environment. The ground floor plan of the house is practically square measuring 15 metres along each side. This line is only broken by two small feeder spouts, in the entrance zone and the

Main facade.

Stain glass window below which is inscribed the name of the building, and detail of the crowning: battlements, chimney and five-armed cross.

other corresponding to the tower-bay window. Its structure is stepped and rises from the entrance to the tower-bay window. This slender tower culminates in a five pointed cross below which a personal interpretation of the Catalan flag is inscribed. The openings to the exterior are not very abundant as would be the case in buildings from the gothic period, and for the same reason all of these are defined by the semi-circular arch.

The fact that this is a privately owned house means that we cannot appreciate the rooms in the house interior where one discovers a very personal Gaudí touch, which is far removed from gothic style exterior. For example, each room has a different ceiling even when they follow the same structure of arches and vaults. The most interesting of these ceilings is the one in the attic which is considered by experts in architecture as one of

the most successful spaces created by Gaudí. Another room of suggestive beauty is the one that comprises the interior patio and the stairway allowing access to the upper floors with its richness of shapes and aesthetic solutions. The entrance railing is also very interesting (a composition in the form of lances in line) and in general the different grilles, likewise made of wrought iron, among many other details.

Rear facade.

Lamp of the interior patio.

Detail of the stain glass window over the main door seen from the inside, made up of an eight-pointed star that continues to the exterior.

Interior patio staircase on the last floor.

View from the attic.

PARK GÜELL

Detail of the pavilion destined to be a porter's lodge. The words «Park» and «Güell» are inscribed on its walls.

PARK GÜELL
(1900-1914). Barcelona.
Municipal Park.

Park Güell began as a private urban planning project assigned to Gaudí by Eusebi Güell along the style of the city gardens that had blossomed in England during that period. It is this link that explains why the park was assigned the name PARK, using the English «K» rather than «C» as in the Catalan «PARC». However, such an ambitious and innovative project did not enjoy the success that was expected as only two of the projected 62 parcels ended up being sold. Despite this, Gaudí was able to finish his work on the park leaving us with a legacy of one of his most suggestive and successful architectural achievements. In 1962 the entire zone

Main entrance to Park Güell.

Park Güell main stairway.

Detail of the stairway: shield of Catalunya and snakehead.

was declared an Artistic Monument by the Local Government of Barcelona, in 1969 the Spanish government declared it a National Monument, and in 1984 UNESCO declared it Heritage to Humanity.

Construction began in 1901 and was set out in three stages. The first stage, between 1901 and 1903, consisted of a levelling of the mountain purchased by Güell which at that time was in the upper part of the small town of Gracia and known as the Montaña Pelada. The purpose of this levelling was to redistribute the terrain to cover an exten-

sion of 15 hectares. The next stage consisted of the construction of the roadways for the internal traffic for this urban area and the planning out of the central levelled area and the lower area of columns set aside for the main recreation plaza and market. The wall protecting the park was built, the entrance pavilions and a show house for a single family to promote the sale of the individual parcels of land.

In the third stage, between 1910 and 1913, the famous undulating bench was built. This stage was to also include the building of various houses, but time

Main stairway: the so-called «dragon of Park Güell» and bench protected from the wind.

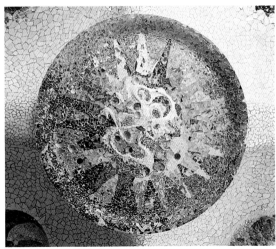

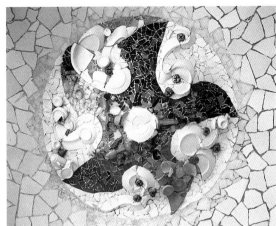

*The Hipóstila Room and three details of the ceiling
decoration, very original collages by
Josep M. Jujol.*

went by and nobody decided to buy any of the lots, basically because the location of this urban development at the beginning of the century was considered to be too far from the city centre, in short, it was too solitary a location. Only two houses were built, one for the lawyer, Martí Trias i Domènech, finished in 1906 according to the plans by the architect Juli Batllevell. The other was purchased by Gaudí himself and also finished in 1906, designed by the architect Francesc Berenguer. Gaudí moved in with the

Details of the decoration of the undulating bench, consists of beautiful «collages» made with pieces of ornamental tiles and other very diverse materials.

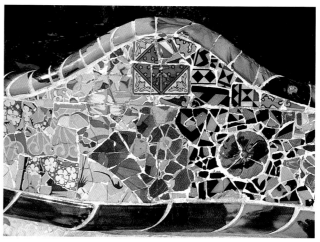

The undulating bench is one of the greatest achievements in Park Güell because its originality and innovativeness.

PARK GÜELL

Aerial view of Park Güell. The large square and lower hall of columns were conceived by Gaudí for housing a large recreational square and a market, respectively, of the development.

little remaining family he had, his father, Francesc, who died at the end of the same year and his niece, Rosa, in delicate health, who passed away in 1912 at the age of 36. Gaudí lived in this house until 1925, the year he decided to move in to the accommodation he had set up in Sagrada Familia. In addition to these two houses we should include a third that was already there when Eusebi Güell bought the land. This house was extended and renovated in 1910 to become the new Güell residence.

These three houses have been preserved to the present day. Güell's house was later fitted out as a municipal school, Gaudí's was later acquired by the association, Friends of Gaudí, and turned into the headquarters for the Gaudí House-Museum containing many items belonging to Gaudí, and the house belonging to Trias i Domènech still belongs to the same family.

The failure of the Park Güell enterprise and the later death of Eusebi Güell in 1918, finally lead Güell's beneficiaries to offer the park to the Local Government de Barcelona in 1922 and so Park Güell passed from a private project to a municipal park.

The main entrance constitutes one of the most fantastic like of the enclosure. The pavilion to the left has a turret crowned by the typical Gaudí five-armed cross and was destined to be the administration centre of the urban area. The pavilion to the right was the porter's lodge. Their unique structure and rich imaginative decoration bestow them more with of a value as a sculpture than as examples of architecture.

The large square hides an ingenious system for collecting rainwater that was designed for supplying the development itself. These waters go down through the inside of the columns to a tank with a capacity of 12,000 m³ that is under the hall of columns.

It has often been commented that they evoke the semblance of houses from the Brothers Grimm fairy tales, especially the story of Hansel and Gretel. The grand flight of steps that opens up behind goes all the way up to the Hipóstila Room. The flight of steps itself is rather solemn, a double structure with platforms over which water falls from a hidden fountain. These platforms are decorated with a medallion with the traditional four bars, insignia of Catalonia, a serpent's head. The other is decorated with another of the well-known dragons of Park Güell. This dragon has a more submissive demeanour than others created by Gaudí. Then, before getting to the Hipóstila Room, there is a curious bench protected from the wind by a concave cuirass.

The most eye-catching element of the Hipóstila Room, whose columns support the large upper plaza, are the false keystones of the vault that decorate the ceiling. For this task, as well as the adornments of the undulating bench in the large plaza, Gaudí relied on the architect Josep Maria Jujol (1879-1949). Jujol was one of Gaudí's preferred disciples who used the leftover ceramics other diverse unused materials to create absolutely beautiful collages. This was to become a forerunner for surrealist and abstract painting some years later.

Next to the large plaza is where the complex network of roadways begins. Some of these were destined to be for wheeled traffic and others for pedestrians. The pedestrian ways are frame structures made of stone originating from the same area and are shaped so that they evoke the surrounding countryside in the manner of a palm tree that opens up into an enormous bush of leaves. The columns and walls are inclined so as to offset the slope at the same time creating fascinating perspectives.

For the pedestrians pathways Gaudí projected curious arched paths with local stones, looking for forms that imitate the surrounding nature.

Gaudí House-Museum.

Gaudí House-Museum: Entrance hall, living room, dining room with furnishings from Casa Batlló, Gaudí's office, Gaudí's bedroom, designed by Gaudí.

Episcopal headquarters, in the Royal Chapel, whose walls were decorated by Gaudí.

MAJORCA CATHEDRAL
(1904-1914). Palma de Mallorca.

Gaudí's participation in the Majorca Cathedral consisted of the entire restoration of the interior to bring it back to its old liturgical spirit. He was hired at the request of the Bishop Campins, of the diocese of Palma de Mallorca, who had met the architect at Sagrada Familia and had been fascinated by Gaudí's knowledge of the ecclesiastical liturgy. However, some of the work remained unfinished when Gaudí finally abandoned the project. As had happened in Astorga in 1914, upon the death of Bishop Campins, discrepancies emerged between the architect and the Cathedral Chapter who were shocked by the vanguard style used by Gaudí and his main collaborator, Josep Maria Jujol. The task of reorganising the interior space basically consisted of: moving the choir from the centre of church to the presbytery, the latter being enlarged; and recovering the large gothic windows and stain glass windows in order to provide the interior with more light. It was precisely the question of illumination that Gaudí studied most. In order to create enough light for each area he designed various lamps and candelabras made from wrought iron, and in many cases applied the use of electric light in a most revolutionary way. Elsewhere, the main baroque altarpiece was eliminated and the square baldachin of the main altarpiece substituted for one that was octagonal in shape and hung from the ceiling. Other items that were the work of Gaudí were part of the furnishings and decorative elements used on the choir-stalls.

General perspective of the main altar with the baldachin suspended from the ceiling.

Crowning of Casa Batlló roof.

CASA BATLLÓ
(1904-1906). Passeig de Gràcia 43, Barcelona.
Privately owned residence.
The main floor, the outer patio and the attic can be visited.

At the same time that Gaudí was working on the Majorca Cathedral and Park Güell (including before finishing the stone viaducts, entrance pavilions and the extraordinary undulating bench of this urban development area), Gaudí was given the assignment of remodelling the house belonging to the Batlló family. This family were another of those wealthy middle class families who operated in the textile industry. Their house was located in the high class district of Gracia just next to the modernist house, Casa Amatller (built between 1898 and 1900 based on the plans by the architect Josep Puig i Cadafalch). The owner, Josep Batlló i Casanovas, had wanted to demolish the already standing building dated 1875 and designed along neoclassical lines and build another. However, Gaudí was against such a decision considering it unnecessary.

And so, leaving the existing structure, lies the great merit of this house. Gaudí designed the two façades (the one facing the street and the rear one, since it is a house between parties), he completely redistributed the ground floor and the main floor (for those who also designed all the furniture), he added the cellars, the attic and the terrace roof, and he united the two interior patios into a much bigger one with the

Main facade.

Crowning of Casa Batlló on the rear facade.

aim of giving priority to natural light and favoring the proper ventilation of the house. It must be noted that this last intervention represented a modernization of the habitat, since little interior light and ventilation prevailed in the apartments during the period of the Barcelonan Eixample. This idea of giving great importance to the interior patio would also be applied to La Pedrera, with the difference that this latter construction was a completely new house.

The result of this design was most surprising and full of fantasy where the freedom of shapes and forms manifest themselves throughout. Put another way, as various experts have pointed out, from this moment on Gaudí applied solutions dictated solely by the evocative character of the environment without the need to resort to any other historical style. In short, he now imposed his original style above all.

One of the most eye-catching aspects of Casa Batlló, as much with the regard to the exterior as the interior, is the almost complete lack of straight lines. It is almost completely covered with undulating shapes beginning with the facade wall itself where polished stone from Montjuïc was employed. Concerning the symbolism of the facade there are various interpretations. For some it is a poetic vision of the sea, for others scenes from Carnaval (identifying the balconies with masks, the polychromatic nature of the wall with the confetti and the original crown with the harlequin's hat). However, probably the most accurate interpretation is that which likens it all to an immense dragon (one of Gaudí's preferred topics) defeated by St. George, patron saint of Catalonia with its symbolic religious transcendence of good overcoming evil. St. George is represented by the lance-tower finished off with a cross plunged into the «spine» of the dragon, whilst the facade is replete with «scales» depicting the dragon with the skulls and bones of its victims. These shapes appear to be inspired by the columns of the first floor and the balconies.

As in all of Gaudí's work even the smallest of details is worthy of mention. We can underline the interior patio in which Gaudí composed an interesting play on light to create a homogenous lighting. There are the ceramics that cover it oscillating between white and a gentle blue becoming more intense as one moves up towards the terrace roof. In this space there is an explosion of colour in the finishings of the chimneys and vent shafts. This same effect is a response to the fact that the window and openings in the interior patio are of different sizes for each floor, larger in the lower floors and smaller in the upper floors.

Of the attic, an impressive space due to it grand elegance and functionality, the organic structure of the parabolic arches, as if they made up the skeleton of an enormous dragon, in which the house is inspired, must be highlighted.

Another detail worth noting are the furnishings that Gaudí designed for the dining room and first floor: doors, lamps, chimneys and many other secondary elements very often integrated into the actual architecture and that, as a whole, constitute the best of Gaudí's interior work. However, today only the front part

Rear facade.

Details of the main facade.

has been preserved of the original owner's flat as the furnishings have now passed into the hands of the Gaudí House-Museum in Park Güell. As was the case in other work carried out by Gaudí, all of these elements were carried out by reputable artisans. Casa i Bardés was assigned the cabinet making, the Badia brothers the wrought iron work, Josep Pelegrí, the glass work, P. Pujol Baucís, son, the tiles, and Sebastià Ribó the ceramics. All of the covering material for the main facade coming from Manacor, Majorca.

Access stairs to the first floor and matching armchair from the old dining room (today in the Park Güell Gaudí House-Museum).
Main floor: entrance hall chimney and a detail of one of the room's ceiling.

View of the facade on the corner oí Passeig de Gràcia.

CASA MILÀ «LA PEDRERA»
(1905-1910). Passeig de Gràcia, 92, Barcelona.
Privately owned living accommodation. Headquarters of the «Fundació Caixa de Catalunya» and «Espai Gaudí».

Whilst Gaudí was finishing the Casa Batlló he accepted a project from the dealer Pere Milà i Camps to design a completely new building as a house also located on Passeig de Gràcia in Barcelona. This was to be his last private building, from 1914 onwards he dedicated himself entirely to Sagrada Familia. The construction of this house took place parallel to the projects Park Güell and the Güell Colony crypt.

This building was immediately baptised by the people of Barcelona, not without certain disdain, with the nickname «Pedrera» which means «a quarry» in Catalan. Also somewhat ironically it was known as «el avispero» (the wasps' nest) and even «la empanada» (the meat pie). These were reactions to the uncertainty that Gaudí's work awoke in public opinion. In the case of this building, he left them in a state of bewilderment as they had never seen anything like it. Many interpret the Casa Milà as a mountain crowned by a great cloud, for others the shapes of its facade were a clear evocation of the rolling sea. There is no doubt that Gaudí took nature as a model and source of inspiration, but it is more than this. It shows the determined will to naturalise architecture, a reverse process to the work done in Park Güell where he architecturalises nature.

96

Detail of the facade on Provença Street.

CASA MILÀ «LA PEDRERA»

Balcony with bars sculpted by Josep M. Jujol.

The initial project for Casa Milà foresaw crowning the building with an enormous group of sculptures dedicated to the Virgin Mary and the baby Jesus in the way of a culmination of the enormous sculpted base that the building is. However, the image it left did not agree with the owner and he turned down the proposal. But, the inscription to Mary «Ave gratia M plena Dominus tecum» was kept along the entire facade in the undulating line that separates the six habitable floors from the two that make up the lofts.

Gaudí also thought of constructing a double spiral ramp around the grand patio that would allow cars and carriages to go up as far as the terrace roof. He finally abandoned the idea and designed the ramps so that they only gained access to the basement whilst he provided for an external spiral staircase in the patio to be able to go up to the living quarters which finally ended up only going as far as the second floor.

The entire Casa Milà site covers 1,620 m² joining two buildings, each one organised around a central patio of curved line shapes. Each one has its own entrance: one on the Passeig de Gràcia and the other opening out on to the Provença street. The entire facade was built with large stone slabs taken from the Garraf and Vilafranca areas and each one cut and placed on site. For the decoration of the railings, all of them different, Gaudí relied on the collaboration of Josep M. Jujol who composed authentic filigrees in wrought iron. The door grilles, designed by Gaudí have quite different lines.

The originality of Casa Milà continues on into the interior, with such innov-

Door to Carrer Provença with grilles drawn by Gaudí.

CASA MILÀ «LA PEDRERA»

Details of the stairway and a roof, and an entranceway to one of the residences.

ative elements such as the already mentioned spiral access ramp leading to the basement for the cars and carriages. Or there is the suppression of the habitual communal staircase typical in the flats in the Eixample area of the city of Barcelona. Instead, Gaudí put forward the idea of allowing access to the floors only by lift or service staircase. In this way he substituted the small and insalubrious ventilation patios for two large interior patios. Likewise, another feature that needs to be pointed out with respect to the interior organisation of the building is that the entire house is supported on columns and a metal framework with no load bearing walls. This allows the space in each flat to be modified for any purpose.

As regards the interior decoration, worth mentioning is the first floor, today an exhibition salon, with columns and ceilings that were the work of Josep Mª Jujol. But, the space that awakens the greatest admiration is the terrace roof. It is made up of a collection of skylights with sinuous shapes where one can find the «Espai Gaudí», over which the terrace roof runs, and the stepped floor populated with unusual sculptures. These original sculptures correspond to the exits from the service stairs (those which carried the main traffic and are

*View of the
interior patio.*

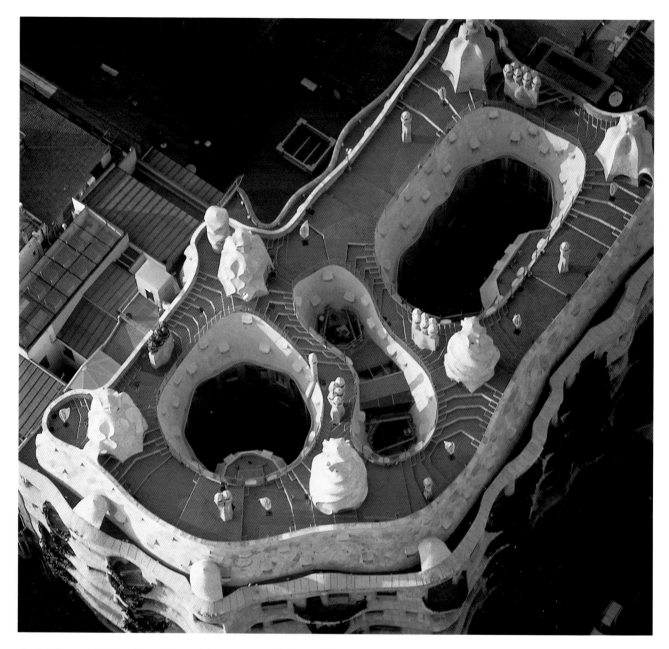

Aerial view of the interior patios and the terrace roof of La Pedrera.

covered with pieces of ceramics), with the vents (those that show multiple holes and whose shapes have been defined as a premonition of abstract sculpture) and with the chimneys (that when seen as a group liken to severe looking hooded guardians).

The Casa Milà was declared an Historic-Artistic Monument by the Spanish State in 1969 and Heritage to Humanity by UNESCO in 1984. In 1986 it was restored by the Fundació de la Caixa de Catalunya who have their headquarters here, fitting out the first floor as an exhibition gallery and the skylights in a space dedicated to the work of Gaudí, the «Espai Gaudí». Since 1999 you can visit the flats in the building which are decorated according to the tastes of the period when the building was built.

«Espai Gaudí»
(Gaudí Space).

Upper part of the patio and terrace roof.

In the Pedrera terrace roof Gaudí created on the those surprising spaces of all of his works.

Outside view of the crypt.

GÜELL COLONY CRYPT
(1895-1915).
Santa Coloma de Cervelló,
Barcelona region.

In 1890, Eusebi Güell, owner of some thirty hectares in Santa Coloma de Cervelló, a town close by Barcelona, founded a large textile complex that included, in addition to the factory and workers' houses, various other items such as gardens, a theatre, cooperatives and a church. But the church soon proved to be too small and so Güell asked Gaudí to build a new church. This was located at the foot of a small mound sur-rounded by a forest of pine trees. Although this assignment was nego-tiated in 1898, the construction work did not begin until 1908 and came to a early halt in 1915. Although the construction remained unfinished (only the crypt and the entrance «portico» were erected) the church was consecrated in 1915.

In order to understand how Gaudí imagined the church would be, var-ious of his sketches and drawing have been preserved, as is the case for Sagrada Familia, but they only give a general idea as to how it was to look. Likewise, and knowing that Gaudí liked to change his ideas and allow them to «mature» at the same time that the construction work was underway, it is difficult to know the final appearance the church would have had in the case of it being fin-ished. In addition, there are no plas-ter models that allow one to guess the shapes used (this was not the case for Sagrada Familia). What is left is a study model that he made to calcu-late the equilibrium forces of the building based on cords that support small sacks filled with pellets with a weight proportional to that which each point had to support. Using this system he was able to obtain a mechanical structure of the building

Entrance to the crypt.

that, seen inverted, demonstrates the resulting spatial effect.

However, the fact that this was an unfinished construction project does not take away the interest the crypt has to offer, in itself it constitutes a masterpiece. As in the case of Park Güell, which was built at the same time as the crypt, Gaudí architecturises nature establishing a close and harmonious link between the building and its environment. This link with nature is expressed in the adaptation of the crypt floor to the hill on which it rests, in the materials used, in the organisation of the columns of the entrance porti-

Stain glass window painted by Josep M. Jujol.

Rear facade.

Interior of the crypt.

co as if it were an extension of the neighbouring pine grove. This can also be seen in each column, being distinct and original the same as trees are in nature, and in the sinuous ribs that are the vaults and roof coverings. Rather than being a work created by a person it really seems that we are entering into a natural grotto, and this peculiarly is not that case because it is not a subterranean building. What helps to give it an effect of darkness is a carefully thought out aesthetics and study of natural light that sifts through very gently via suggested and colourful stain glass windows.

The rounded shapes of the four central columns of the crypt also surprise the eye, achieved through a simple juxtaposition of large stone slabs. Likewise, worthy of mention is the collection of benches which combine metal and wood.

Model made of cords and small sacks of pellets to calculate the equilibrium forces of the building.

111

CONTENTS

EDITORIAL ESCUDO DE ORO, S.A.
Palaudàries, 26 - 08004 Barcelona
Tel: 93 230 86 10 - E-mail: editorial@eoro.com